T0086071

JEREMY LIN RISING STAR

James Buckley Jr.

SCHOLASTIC INC.

New York   Toronto   London   Auckland
Sydney   Mexico City   New Delhi   Hong Kong

Dedicated to Dalton, the best basketball player I know!
—JB

Front cover photo: © Jim Mone/ASSOCIATED PRESS

Inside front cover top: © Bill Kostroun/ASSOCIATED PRESS;
bottom: © Frank Franklin II/ASSOCIATED PRESS

Inside back cover top: © Seth Wenig/ASSOCIATED PRESS;
bottom: © Kathy Willens/ASSOCIATED PRESS

© 2012 by Scholastic Inc.

ISBN 978-0-545-49147-1

Published by Scholastic Inc.
SCHOLASTIC and associated logos are trademarks and/or registered trademarks of Scholastic Inc.

12 11 10 9 8 7 6 5 4 3 2 1   12 13 14 15 16/0
Printed in the U.S.A.   40
First printing, April 2012

CONTENTS:

Introduction

On February 3, 2012, only a small handful of die-hard basketball fans had ever heard of Jeremy Lin. He was on less than one percent of Americans' fantasy basketball teams.

On February 4, he came off the bench to lead the New York Knicks to a big win. New Yorkers were now paying attention.

On February 6, he got his first start in more than two years as an NBA player . . . and led the Knicks to another victory while scoring a career-high 28 points and playing almost 45 minutes of that game.

Almost overnight, everyone in sports knew Jeremy Lin. What's more, thanks to his Asian-American heritage, he was becoming a celebrity in the world's biggest country—China.

By February 10, he had become an international sensation, outscoring Kobe Bryant when the Knicks beat the L.A. Lakers.

And on it went, game after game, win after win, as what was almost immediately named "Linsanity" continued to grow. Fans who thought they had seen it all found themselves watching something new every night. Opponents who figured they could teach this kid from Harvard a thing or two discovered that he was the one doing the schooling. He won games with late free throws and last-second three-pointers. He threw perfect no-look passes for alley-oops. He made steals from some of the league's best point guards. Jeremy was a one-man, do-it-all basketball wrecking crew.

But what made Jeremy's sudden stardom so amazing was not so much what he was doing, but how he had gotten there. He had not gone to a big basketball college, he had not been drafted by the NBA, and he had been cut by two teams only a month before he hit it big.

As he led the Knicks to win after win, amazed fans from around the world had one question: Where did this guy come from?

First Bounce

The story of how Jeremy Lin became the biggest thing to hit basketball since the slam dunk starts in far-off Taiwan. That island nation, located off the coast of China, is the homeland of Gie-Ming and Shirley Lin. The Lin family was originally from mainland China, in the province of Fujian. But Gie-Ming's family had lived in Taiwan since the early 1700s.

Gie-Ming's father was a translator who spoke several languages. Education was central to their lives, and Gie-Ming studied at Taiwan's top university. After learning about electrical engineering, he was invited to move to Virginia by a former teacher. Though Gie-Ming didn't speak any English, he seized the opportunity. While working, he also attended Old Dominion University for an advanced degree. He met a fellow student there and they soon fell in love and married. Wu Xinxin, who later changed her name to Shirley, was also from Taiwan and studied computer science.

The couple moved several times but settled in California, where they had three boys. Neither Gie-Ming nor Shirley are very tall, but both had high hopes for themselves and their sons. They were also fascinated by something else in America: basketball. Gie-Ming loved to watch NBA stars like Larry Bird, Kareem Abdul-Jabbar, and Julius "Dr. J" Erving on TV. He studied their moves and was impressed with how they worked hard and competed to be the best at this exciting sport.

In 1993, Gie-Ming and Shirley settled in Palo Alto, California. Home to Stanford University, Palo Alto is about 30 miles south of San Francisco.

Gie-Ming decided that he would teach the three boys—Josh, Jeremy, and Joseph—this new game that he loved. He had started to play a little bit himself. (His friends said his favorite shot was the sky hook.) He knew there was only one way to learn—start at the bottom and work hard.

So the family started regular visits to the YMCA near their house.

"I realized if I brought them from a young age it would be like second nature for them," Gie-Ming said. "If they had the fundamentals, the rest would be easy."

Jeremy's grandmother Lin Chu A Muen often visited from her home in Taiwan. She helped to take care of her grandsons and would feed them fried rice with dried turnips to give them the energy to practice for hours.

"My son, when he came home from work, would always take the kids to play basketball," said Grandma Lin. "He took Jeremy to the basketball courts as soon as he could walk."

Jeremy didn't mind all the hard work. For him, it was playtime.

In 2010, he told interviewer Tim Dalrymple, "When I first started playing basketball, I was five years old, and my dad put a ball in my hands. Ever since I was a little kid, I just loved to play this game. I was always in the gym. I loved playing. That's what I did for fun, all the time."

Jeremy's older brother, Josh, has a slightly different memory of Jeremy's early days on the court. He told *Time* magazine, "[Jeremy] stood at half-court sucking his thumb for about half his games that season." After Shirley stopped going to his games, Jeremy realized he had to do his best to get his mom to watch. When she finally came back to see him play, Jeremy led the team in scoring. After that he played hard in every game.

Gie-Ming kept at it, taking the boys to the gym every night after they finished their homework. All the years Gie-Ming spent watching NBA stars paid off. He helped his sons learn the game from the best players in the world. They practiced how to shoot like Larry Bird, the amazing Boston Celtics star who had an awesome three-pointer. They learned dribbling from Dr. J, one of the most exciting players in the game. They even practiced the sky hook like Los Angeles Lakers legend Kareem Abdul-Jabbar.

Jeremy and his brothers started playing on teams at the YMCA and moved on to teams in the National Junior Basketball league. In fact, Jeremy was in sixth grade when Shirley led a group of parents to bring an NJB league to their town, in part so her boys could have skilled competition. The Lin boys were all hoops-crazy, playing on every team they could.

Pete Diepenbrock, who would later coach Jeremy in high school, said, "Jeremy was a youth league legend."

Josh Lin was the oldest by two years and the first to go to high school. He immediately joined the school's basketball team. He played for Gunn High in Palo Alto. Jeremy tagged along to many of the team practices, running sprints with the big boys. He also sometimes worked as a scorekeeper during Josh's games.

Jeremy knew that he wanted to have basketball in his life. He could play the game, he knew all the moves, and he was willing to work hard at it. He loved basketball so much that his room was covered with posters of the players he worshipped. Some of them played for the nearby Golden State Warriors, one of Jeremy's favorite teams growing up.

After years of watching Josh play, Jeremy was finally headed to high school himself. But he had one problem. He was still shorter than his 5-6 dad. Jeremy Lin, the basketball-crazy kid, was going to be too short to play in high school.

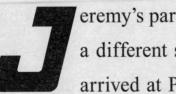

High-School Success

Jeremy's parents chose to send him to a different school than Josh. Jeremy arrived at Palo Alto High School as a freshman in 2002, ready to take the school and its basketball team by storm. "But I went into high school at five foot three inches, one-hundred-and-twenty-five pounds, and every day I came home from practice asking my parents if I would grow taller. Physically, I was so far behind. I was just trying to make the team!"

The coaches saw past his size, however, and he earned a spot on the junior varsity team as a freshman. (JV teams are usually made up of freshmen and sophomores.) In fact, his freshman coach said later that Jeremy had more ability than anyone he'd ever seen.

When the varsity team made the playoffs, that coach, Pete Diepenbrock, brought Jeremy up to help out.

"He nailed a key three-pointer down the stretch of his first game," Diepenbrock said. "He never stopped making them. Even as a five-three, one-hundred-twenty-five-pound freshman, Jeremy lived and breathed basketball. And more than that, he knew he was the best on any court we stepped on."

As a sophomore, Jeremy, who had grown several inches between seasons, made the varsity team. He was named sophomore of the year. He even dunked for the first time. The first person he told about the big moment? His father, Gie-Ming, the man who had worked so hard to teach Jeremy the game they loved.

Jeremy started to get better, but his effort dropped off. He was having so much success that he thought he knew it all. Coach Diepenbrock noticed that he wasn't working as hard in practice. If Jeremy was going to keep improving, something had to change. Unfortunately, he learned that lesson in a painful way.

"I was always one of the better players and that fed my ego," he told a "First Person" interviewer on Palo Alto Online in late 2011. "I felt like I knew everything and didn't need any help. But then I broke my ankle junior year and that changed everything. After that, I realized that the game is a gift that I could lose at any moment if I had an injury. I changed my attitude, listened to my coaches, and started to really work harder."

Jeremy bounced back from that broken ankle to help his team win 32 of 34 games in his junior year. That set a school record for most victories in a season.

Jeremy wasn't just all about basketball in high school. He was also editor of the school newspaper. He studied hard enough to post a 4.2 GPA. In the summer before his senior year, he had an internship with a California state senator. All of these other activities taught Jeremy about how important it was for him to have interests and skills beyond just basketball.

Heading into his senior year in 2005, and having grown to be 6-2, Jeremy knew that he would need to have another great season if he wanted to gain the attention of college coaches and be offered scholarships. If he did, it would pay for the cost of going to college and he could keep playing basketball. With Jeremy's skills, he had a great shot at getting one.

All season long, Jeremy made big plays to lead his team to wins. He had per-game averages of 15 points, seven assists, six rebounds, and five steals for the season.

In an early December game, Palo Alto trailed by a point late in overtime. Jeremy's three-pointer gave the team a two-point win. A few weeks later, his clutch assist led to the game-tying basket in another overtime victory. Later on in the month, Jeremy clinched a key tournament win with a steal and two foul shots in the final seconds of the game.

Palo Alto won 32 of their 33 games that season. They earned the right to move up to a statewide tournament. As the Northern

HOOPS TALK

Averages: Most basketball player stats are shown as per-game averages. For example, if a player has 100 points in 10 games, he has a 10 points-per-game average.

Percentages: Shooting stats are shown as another kind of percentage. If a player takes 10 three-point shots and makes four of them, his number is .400, meaning he made 40 percent of those type of shots.

California champs, they took on Southern California champs, Mater Dei from Santa Ana, in the California Division II state title game. That team was ranked among the very best in the entire country. They had dominated that season in Southern California and had several players who were headed to big college programs. But Mater Dei didn't have Jeremy Lin. He was the star of the game, scoring 17 points.

Rebounds: When a shot is missed, the ball is up for grabs. The player who snags the ball for his team gets credit for a rebound.

Assist: A pass to a teammate who then immediately scores is called an assist.

Steal: When a player knocks the ball away from an opponent and gets control of the ball for his own team.

Diepenbrock described the final moments of that huge win: "We're up two in the final thirty seconds. Jeremy decides to drive to the basket. He takes on their star [Taylor King], goes over him to make a layup to ice it."

The opposing coach recognized the star that had just beaten his team. "The kid makes everyone around him way better," Mater Dei coach Gary McKnight said. "He was very impressive."

Following that magical senior season, Jeremy won several prestigious awards. He was named the Northern California Player of the Year by two newspapers. He made the California All-State team. And he was also the Northern California Scholar-Athlete of the Year, an award given to a person who excels in the classroom and in sports.

Jeremy fully expected to be offered scholarships to play college ball. His high grades and his outstanding basketball skills should have made him much sought after. He didn't want to just go anywhere that asked, however. He wanted a school that was the right fit for him, in the classroom and on the court.

"Academics were very important, so the schools I was looking at were all pretty good academically," Jeremy told Hornets.com. "From there, it was 'Which one would I be able to play basketball for?' Harvard and Brown were the two schools that really wanted me to go [play basketball]. Stanford and UCLA were my dream schools, but that didn't work out [athletically]."

Amazingly, no schools offered him a

scholarship. Jeremy even made a DVD of his high-school highlights and mailed it along with a letter about himself to all the schools he wanted to play for. None sent back the answers he wanted.

"The Pac-10 schools wanted me to walk on," Jeremy remembered. "The Ivy League schools, Harvard and Brown, were the two ones that really wanted me to go there and play for them. I was deciding mainly between those two conferences. I didn't really want to walk on. I wanted to go somewhere the team wanted me, not somewhere I'd have to go and potentially not have a spot on the team."

To "walk on" meant that he was not guaranteed a spot on the team. He could attend the school without a scholarship and show up to try out for basketball. But the chances were high that he would either not make the team, or he'd make it and hardly ever get a chance to play in games. For a player who had won so many awards and so many games, it was a very sad ending to his high-school years.

Rex Walters, a former NBA player who now coaches at the University of San Francisco and watched Jeremy play in high school, said, "Most colleges start recruiting a guy in the first five minutes they see him because he runs really fast, jumps really high, does the quick, easy thing to evaluate. Jeremy's the kind of player you have to see for a while to appreciate."

"I just think in order for someone to understand my game," Jeremy said later, "they have to watch me more than once, because I'm not going to do anything that's extra flashy or freakishly athletic."

Whatever the reasons, Jeremy saw his dreams being crushed.

"At that time I was obviously pretty upset," Jeremy said. "I felt like I deserved a little more, but that put a chip on my shoulder and it pushed me to work really, really hard. It was a blessing in disguise."

That blessing came in a place not normally known for great basketball, but certainly known as one of the finest colleges in the world. Fortunately, Jeremy had worked just as hard in the classroom as he did on the court. His great grades made it possible for him to head east to Harvard University.

At Harvard

Founded in 1636, Harvard University is the oldest college in the United States. Seven U.S. presidents have attended the school, as have dozens of other world leaders. Just getting into Harvard means you're a special student, so Jeremy was not really disappointed to be attending such a wonderful place. However, while Harvard has turned out some of the world's most successful people in business, law, government, and science, it is not exactly a basketball powerhouse.

The Harvard Crimson had never won an Ivy League title. The last Harvard player to make it to the NBA was named Ed Smith, and it was in 1953! Jeremy had beat the odds by becoming a young star even though he was only 5-3 as a freshman in high school. He had made it to the top as an all-star and a state champ . . . but now he was starting all over again—a freshman on a team that didn't win a lot at a school where basketball barely registered with students.

But Jeremy, who had grown to his current height of 6-3, loves a challenge and was determined to change people's minds. When he was a freshman at Harvard in 2006, one of the coaches told him that he was one of the "weakest Harvard basketball players . . . ever." That inspired Jeremy to start lifting weights, knowing that being stronger would make him a better basketball player.

Freshmen don't play on the varsity team at Harvard, so he spent his first season practicing with the team and working on his studies. However, one of the coaches saw something in Jeremy's skills and attitude that had a huge impact on the young player. Assistant coach Kenny Blakeney told him, "You have a shot to play in the NBA."

This was the first time someone had told Jeremy that. He had dreamed of it in the back of his mind. But after not getting a scholarship offer and ending up at Harvard, an NBA career seemed highly unlikely. Blakeney and Jeremy were probably the only two people who thought it was still possible.

Jeremy quickly got to work on making that dream come true. As a sophomore he started to play regularly, and the Crimson were winning games. But this success led to another important challenge in Jeremy's life.

For the first time, he faced the sting of racism. As an Asian-American, Jeremy was not an unusual sophomore at Harvard. As a college basketball player, however, he was almost one-of-a-kind. Only a small handful of Asian-Americans were playing college hoops at the time. Opposing fans started making fun of Jeremy's race. They would yell things out during games to try and distract him. Jeremy faced this with the same poise and determination as everything else he had overcome.

"I'm naturally competitive and cocky," he told Tim Dalrymple in 2010. "I love proving people wrong. I love competing. When I first started hearing those [racist] remarks, I would always want to say something back, or to play well to get them back. As I grew older, I realized that I shouldn't allow that stuff to affect me, and at the same time I shouldn't retaliate. I shouldn't say anything back. So at this point, now, this year, it hasn't really bothered me. It's just something I'm used to now."

The flip side of being an Asian-American athlete was that Jeremy quickly got a lot of positive attention from Asian-American fans. They would come out to games just to see him in action. Jeremy loved seeing so many cheering fans; their enthusiasm and support gave him a shot of energy at every game.

In the 2008–09 season, as a junior, he was the only hoopster in the nation to rank in the top 10 in his conference in every major stat category. He led the Ivy League in scoring (17.8 points per game), rebounds (5.5 per game), and even three-point percentage (.400). All those skills that he had worked on with his dad were coming into play.

The biggest game of his junior year came against crosstown rival Boston College. (Cambridge, Harvard's home, is just across the river from Boston.) B.C. had just knocked off the number-one team in the country the week before they played Harvard, so they were moving up the rankings. Then, in an incredible performance, Jeremy poured in 27 points, had eight assists, and pulled down six rebounds. The Crimson stunned the Eagles and won 82–70. It was one of the biggest wins in recent Harvard history.

At the start of the 2009–10 season, Jeremy's last at Harvard, the national media was finally starting to pay attention. Jeremy was honored that ESPN.com named him one of the most versatile players in the country before his senior season. In November, against William & Mary, Harvard played one of its most dramatic games of the season. The two teams were tied and went to overtime . . . again and again! It went all the way to three overtime periods. Finally, the exhausted Crimson players looked to their leader to save them . . . and he did. Just as the final overtime period ended, Jeremy launched a 40-foot shot that went in to win the game.

"He's as good an all-around guard as I've seen," said William & Mary coach Tony Shaver after that game. "He's a special player who seems to have a special passion for the game. I wouldn't be surprised to see him in the NBA one day."

The NBA. More and more people were starting to think that dream might come true for Jeremy.

College and NBA coaches took notice of Jeremy even when his team lost to No. 14-ranked Connecticut. He had 30 points and nine rebounds as Harvard fell by only six points. The Connecticut coach said about Jeremy, "I can't think of a team that he wouldn't play for."

Back home, nobody was prouder than Jeremy's father. Gie-Ming watched the whole game and marveled at the superstar athlete his son had become. They'd come a long way from the YMCA. "Every time he did something good, they'd play it over and over again," Gie-Ming said. "I kept watching, and they kept showing him."

For his part, Jeremy's coach had the best view of anyone—and Tommy Amaker knew what he was talking about. Amaker had been a star college player at powerful Duke University. He later coached at top Division I schools Seton Hall and Michigan.

"Jeremy has been one of the better players in the country for a while now," Amaker said.

"He's as consistent as anyone in the game. People who haven't seen him are wowed by what they see, but we aren't. What you see is who he is."

The odds remained long that even with all his Harvard success Jeremy would make the NBA. The pro league hadn't looked at Harvard for a player in more than 50 years. The last player to make the NBA from any Ivy League school was Chris Dudley of Yale, way back in 1987.

As his Harvard career ended and the 2010 NBA Draft neared, could Jeremy defy the odds and continue his move up the basketball ladder?

Another Hurdle

When Harvard's season ended in March 2010, Jeremy returned to the life of a full-time student. He continued to attend his classes in order to graduate in June with a degree in economics. Even if the NBA didn't work out for him, his Harvard education was extremely valuable. (On his YouTube channel, he posted a funny video that he made with friends called "How to Get Into Harvard.")

Before he put that degree to work, he wanted to take a shot at his pro basketball dream. On June 24, 2010, the NBA held its annual draft. The draft allows NBA teams to choose new players to add to their rosters. Most of the time the players come from colleges, but sometimes players from overseas are chosen as well.

Jeremy watched the draft eagerly. He didn't think he was going to hear his name called in the first round. (He was good, but not that good!) He knew that playing at Harvard was not in his favor, either. The draft only lasts two rounds and Jeremy hoped to be one of the 64 players chosen.

He wasn't.

"I thought I was going to be borderline—could potentially [get drafted], could potentially not get drafted," Jeremy said later. "It was obviously a very disappointing night for me, but looking back, it was the best situation for me, because I was able to be a free agent and to take offers from different teams."

Jeremy is exactly the kind of person to take a disappointment and turn it into something he could overcome. Not being drafted was just another issue for him to triumph over.

The first step was to attract NBA teams looking to add more players as free agents. A player who is not drafted can sign with any team that makes him an offer.

In order to showcase his talents, Jeremy

joined the NBA's "summer league" in Las Vegas in early July 2010. He was trying to figure out what kind of player he was and what he could do to improve enough to catch the eye of an NBA team.

At the time, talking with HoopsDaily.com, he compared himself to a player on the Phoenix Suns with a similar style. "I see myself more as a Goran Dragic type of point guard. We both love attacking the rim, effectively using the pick-and-roll, and playing with high basketball IQ, although neither of us are freak athletes. Because I also played some shooting guard in college, I have the ability to play that position well."

During the summer-league games, Jeremy was put on a team with players from all over

Point guard: The player who dribbles the ball up the court. He runs the offense on most teams. He passes to teammates, calls plays, and also tries to score.

Shooting guard: This player has to shoot well from the outside and play tight defense. He can also look for chances to drive to the basket.

Pick-and-roll: An important play in which a player screens a defender, or "sets a pick," then moves, or "rolls," quickly to the side, becoming open for a pass and an easy bucket.

the country and sent out to play. Scouts and coaches watched . . . and learned. In the last of five games that he played, Jeremy faced off against John Wall from Kentucky. He had been the number-one pick of the Washington Wizards and had won several national player-of-the-year awards in college.

As would be the case many times in his future, Jeremy took advantage of an opportunity. He was ready when fellow guard Rodrigue Beaubois was hurt in that game. That meant that Jeremy got to play against Wall quite a lot more than planned.

Jeremy made the most of his chance. He showed off all the versatility he'd been famous for in college. The crowd loved it. Jeremy's surprising energy outshone Wall, even though Wall was the much more famous player.

Later, Jeremy told Hornets.com, "Summer league was, 'Five games, show what you can do.' Obviously, the biggest one for me was against John Wall, and I'm just thankful to God that it worked out that way. It was part of a plan where all of these different things had to happen and eventually I got a chance to play against John Wall. Then I have my best quarter in the fourth quarter of that last game."

Along with summer league, Jeremy had private workouts with the Oklahoma City Thunder, Los Angeles Lakers, New York Knicks, Memphis Grizzlies, and San Antonio Spurs. They all wanted to see what he could do. Several teams even made him small offers to join.

One of those offers was especially interesting. Dallas Mavericks Coach Donnie Nelson had been the one to invite Jeremy to Las Vegas a week before the summer league even started. He took Jeremy out to dinner and made him feel comfortable around all the top players.

"Donnie took care of me. He really took care of me," Jeremy remembered. "He really, really did. I'm not just saying that. And I'm really thankful to him. It was tough [to tell Nelson no], obviously, because I was there for ten days before the summer-league training. And I had met with Donnie back in March or April."

But in the end, Nelson would be disappointed. On July 21, 2010, Jeremy got a call from his agent, Roger Montgomery. They had been given an offer by the Golden State Warriors, and they had accepted it.

When he got the call, Jeremy said later, "I just remember saying, 'I can't believe this!' I was yelling. I was fist pumping. I was screaming. I can't remember all that I said, but if you were anywhere near my house, you probably would have heard me."

His dream had come true. Jeremy Lin was an NBA player. And to make it even sweeter, the Warriors played in Oakland, just across San Francisco Bay from Jeremy's Palo Alto home.

Jeremy didn't know it at the time, but he had a secret admirer in the Warriors' front office. Joe Lacob was the new owner of the team. Having lived in the area for many years, Lacob was well versed about the hometown hero, as he told the *San Jose Mercury News*:

"There were probably three guys that were pretty much the best point guards in high school in this [San Francisco] area at that time and Jeremy Lin was probably the best of them. And my son [Kirk] was right there with him. I've watched them play against each other and I've coached against him since he was this high. So I know him from a little kid. Also at Palo Alto I watched him win the state championship over a superior team, and he dominated it. And he has heart, he has a lot of talent, he's athletic, which a lot of people don't understand. He has a game that translates to the NBA. He can drive, he's a slasher."

Jeremy had become the first Asian-American to play in the NBA since 1947. Other players had had one Asian-American or Asian parent, and several were native to China, but Jeremy was unique. He was a young man born and raised in the U.S., by Asian parents, playing professional basketball!

Jeremy's first press conferences were filled

with reporters from around the country. At road games in the preseason, Asian-American fans helped pack arenas. Wrote reporter Matt Wong of ESPN.com after an early-season game, "Despite playing only three minutes on this night, [Jeremy's] impact on the game was deeper than he might realize: He has captured the imagination of many Asian-American fans around the country. Including mine."

Jeremy was aware of his position in that community and it was one he took seriously.

"There's a lot of publicity in terms of being an Asian-American player, but my heritage means a lot to me," he said. "I'm very proud to be of Asian heritage and I just want to reach my potential as a player."

He was also attracting a lot of international

attention. Basketball is very popular in China and Taiwan. Fans there were very excited to see someone of their heritage making it into the NBA. Only a year earlier, the most famous Chinese-born player ever, Houston center Yao Ming, retired due to foot injuries. Yao had been an enormous international star. He was selected to eight All-Star Games in large part thanks to votes cast online by fans in China. Only soccer rivals basketball for international popularity, and in China, basketball is number one.

With Yao out of the NBA, Jeremy immediately became a new hero for hoops-loving fans in the world's biggest country. TV networks from across Asia sent reporters to follow Jeremy's new pro career.

Some of those fans got to see Jeremy in

person. In the summer, before he reported to the Warriors' training camp, the Lin family was invited to visit Taiwan. Yao Ming asked the new NBA rookie to take part in a charity game there. Jeremy took the chance to visit his parents' home country and to take them with him.

BASKETBALL PIONEER

The first Asian-American in the NBA played in the league's second season. Wat Misaka, born in Utah but of Japanese heritage, was drafted by the Knicks after starring for the University of Utah. Only 5-7, he had impressed the New York crowd when he played very well in a college tournament. The Knicks remembered and chose him in the draft. He only played three games with the team, however. He left basketball soon after and had a long career as an engineer.

While there, he was asked if he would play for Taiwan's national team someday. (With parents who were born in Taiwan, he would qualify for the team.) He said decisions like that were down the line for him; he wanted to focus on his pro career first. He played in the game and enjoyed spending time with the young Taiwanese players at a youth camp.

At the first preseason game played in Oakland, Jeremy got the biggest ovation of the night when he came into the game in the fourth quarter.

"That really touched me. It's something I'll remember forever," Lin said. "This whole opportunity is a blessing from God, and I'm very thankful for that. To get to play in front of so many family and friends, it's pretty indescribable."

Of course, since he was a rookie, it was up to his teammates to make him feel like part of the team. After scoring seven points in the game and finishing his visits with reporters, Jeremy headed to the locker room to clean up. He had one problem, though: His teammates had hidden all his shoes.

His coach made sure that he didn't get a big head, either. In practices, no fouls against Jeremy were ever called. "He's tough as nails," said Coach Keith Smart. "I thought it was necessary for him to understand that as a no-name guy, you won't get any favors. So you've got to work through all that. And he's done that."

The attention Jeremy got from the hometown fans sometimes backfired. Early in his rookie season, he often tried too hard when playing at home, and his teammates noticed.

"He was kind of unfazed on the court, and there is no doubt that he plays hard and tries to make the right plays," guard Stephen Curry told the *San Francisco Chronicle*. "There's a lot of pressure on him at home, with all of the applause for just checking into the game, so I'm sure that cranks his nerves up a little bit. You can tell on the road he plays a lot better, because he can just go out there, play, and have fun."

Once the regular season started, Jeremy didn't see much action. The Warriors had veteran guards in Curry and Monta Ellis. Jeremy was just a rookie third-stringer, and he knew it. He continued to get attention from fans, however. On October 29, 2010, he made his NBA debut. He entered the game late in the fourth quarter and the fans at Oracle Arena gave him a standing ovation. The crowd was packed in for Asian Heritage Night, one of several special evenings that teams hold to honor different groups of fans. Many in this crowd were especially proud to see Jeremy take the court.

The next game, against the Lakers, he got his first NBA points and also had four steals in 11 minutes of playing time. But he showed he was still learning, as he committed five fouls.

After the game, which the Warriors lost, he showed that he knew how far he had to go. "I'm not going to really talk about what I did personally when we lost by twenty-four. I'm just learning slowly the NBA game. There's not one specific thing that I might have learned in between one game and the next, but this experience to be able to get out on the floor and stay comfortable was helpful."

Like the fans packing Oracle Arena, some opponents were noticing Lin's play. The veteran point guard Derek Fisher of the Lakers said this after their win over Golden State: "He plays with good energy on the floor. He's aggressive. He plays hard. He's not afraid of the competition. Those are good things to have when you're a young player regardless of where you're from. You have to be willing to go out there and compete against the best." This kind of energetic play made him and his fans think bright things were ahead.

Basketball Ups and Downs

After the excitement of the start of his first NBA season, Jeremy slowly adjusted to the busy daily life of a pro player. The team held practices on off-days, while they had shootarounds on game days. He also had to travel a lot more often. The team flew around the country to play in places such as Toronto, Houston, Salt Lake City, and Phoenix.

As a backup, Jeremy's minutes were still limited, but on November 21, against the Lakers, he had his most points in any game during his rookie season, scoring 13 in 18 minutes of action.

Jeremy remembered the lesson he had learned in high school: Just because you've made it doesn't mean you can stop working. Jeremy was always the first to practice, sometimes arriving three hours before the rest of the team so he could get in extra shooting, which impressed Coach Smart. Jeremy would also study videos of the best guards in the league to try and improve his game.

Throughout November and December, Jeremy worked hard and waited for his turn to get playing time. He rarely ever played more than a few minutes. Golden State was struggling as a team. They had only won once from November 21 through December 20.

That certainly wasn't Jeremy's fault, but the coaches knew that he would not improve without consistent minutes. To get those minutes, Jeremy was sent down to the team's NBA Development League (or D-League) team in Reno, Nevada. It was a hard thing for him to deal with at first. He had finally seen his NBA dreams come true, only to find himself in what was basically the minor leagues of basketball.

"To be honest, I was struggling with it," Jeremy told NBA.com about the team's decision. "I felt like I was being demoted or not good enough to play in the NBA."

Instead of moping, Jeremy saw the silver

lining. With Reno, he would play full games as well as get extra practice time. He'd be with coaches who had more time for him, since he'd be one of the team's starters.

Jeremy could say about his time in Reno, "Now it's changed my perspective. I wouldn't be able to put this work in with the Warriors. I'm just trying to learn and grow until I'm ready for the Warriors to call me back up."

Jeremy was a star player for the D-League Reno Bighorns. He averaged 18 points, 5.8 rebounds, and 4.3 assists in 20 games.

Coach Eric Musselman, a longtime NBA coach, saw something special in Jeremy during their time together in Reno. He saw a player eager to learn and to improve.

"He had no problems scoring for himself,"

Musselman told the *New York Times*. "It was more seeing the opposite side of the floor, and using the whole floor, instead of just the side the pick-and-roll was on. And he kept getting better and better at that."

At a special all-star "Showcase" event played in January, Jeremy was named to the tournament First Team after averaging 21.5 points and 6.0 rebounds per game. In another game for Reno, he poured in 27 points, including making 13 out of 14 free-throw attempts.

"Being able to come down here has been a blessing in disguise for me," he said. "It's been huge for my development as a player so I'm trying to try to take advantage of it."

Jeremy showed off his generosity, too. When the Bighorns flew from city to city for games, Jeremy got a first-class seat since he was officially on an NBA team. But he usually gave that nicer seat to a teammate and sat in back with the rest of the team.

All that extra work in Reno paid off. Jeremy was called back to the Warriors in February 2011. (He later had two shorter visits to Reno.) His playing time increased a little bit, but he was still not more than a backup. However, in an April game against the NBA champions of that season, the Dallas Mavericks, Jeremy came off the bench to provide an important spark. The Warriors trailed by 10 points when Jeremy first took the floor. He only had four points, but his leadership and hustle inspired the team. By the time he subbed out and the starters came back in, the Warriors trailed by just a point. They went on to post an upset win, 99–92. With the Warriors out of the playoff race, Jeremy got more and more minutes late in the season, reaching a season-high 24 minutes in a game against Portland. In that game, which would be the final one he played as an NBA rookie, Jeremy also made his first NBA three-point shot.

What he didn't know was that it was the last game he would play for his hometown team.

As Jeremy headed into his first off-season, he and the entire NBA were in for a shock. Just a few days after the end of the 2010–11 season, the NBA closed.

It was officially called a lockout. Players couldn't practice with their teammates or be trained by their coaches. Teams could not sign new players or re-sign the players that they already had.

Just because there was no NBA season didn't mean Jeremy was done working. During the lockout, he headed home to Palo Alto and did almost nothing but play hoops. He worked out with a pickup team put together by his former coach Diepenbrock. He hired a coach named Doc Scheppler to help him improve his three-point shooting. Scheppler had actually coached Diepenbrock in high school.

Scheppler taught Jeremy a game called "Beat the Ghost." When Jeremy made a shot outside the three-point stripe, he got a point. When he missed, the "ghost" got three points! He shot and shot until he could "beat the ghost."

"That's the beauty of Jeremy Lin,"

Scheppler said. "It's not about moral victories. It's 'I have to win.'" Scheppler told the *San Jose Mercury News*, "That's the lesson here: If you don't like the way things are going for you in a sport, don't cry about it. Don't whine to the coach. Do something about it."

Working with Scheppler, Jeremy took 500 to 600 shots in 90-minute sessions. They would meet several times a week.

Jeremy also worked on his conditioning with trainer Phil Wagner. Together they improved his agility and leaping ability. Jeremy also continued to lift weights and gained several pounds of muscle by working with E.J. Costello at a Bay Area gym.

Jeremy's typical daily summer workout schedule went something like this:

7–9 a.m.:	Five-on-five basketball
10–11 a.m.:	Agility training
11–noon:	Weight training
1–2 p.m.:	Shooting work
2–4 p.m.:	Individual work

Jeremy also took time during his off-season to give back to the community that had supported him for so long. He told "First Person," "During the lockout time, I started the Lin Foundation and my YouTube channel. For the foundation, my whole goal is to use the platform that I've been blessed with to impact other people. I have a strong desire to help underprivileged or homeless youth. That's where I'm trying to go with it, we're just experimenting right now and finding organizations to partner with."

Meanwhile, the talks between NBA owners and players went on. The league canceled games in October. Many players wanted to keep playing, so they looked to leagues in other countries. Jeremy found a perfect place to play: China. He was asked by Coach Brian Goorjian to come play a few games for the Dongguan Leopards, a team based in southern China.

Goorjian saw what other coaches had seen for years: a hardworking, first-class player and person. As he told the Australian newspaper *The Age*, "No attitude, wants to work, wants to get better, very dedicated, very strong, very quick, and a lot of talent, obviously. It was his mind-set when he got there. He'd come each day for shots with me in the morning before the game, he'd train with us and he'd meet us and drive over, then he'd go back with his parents and stay in a hotel."

In August 2011, Jeremy helped the team win four games and make it to the finals of a tournament, where he was named most valuable player. He was later asked to consider joining the Chinese Basketball Association full-time while the NBA was in its lockout. Jeremy, however, said he had a contract with the Warriors and graciously turned down the offer.

By the fall, as the lockout continued, that full-time job was looking less likely. In late November, Jeremy was talking with Teramo Basket, a team in Italy, about playing there. He had to keep playing somewhere to stay sharp.

Then came great news: The lockout was over! The NBA and its players finally agreed on a new deal. The players were headed back to the court in just a few days. Jeremy was ready to take on the league. With his shooting improved and with all the hard work he had put in over the summer, he knew that he was a better player than he had been during his rookie season. He just needed a chance to prove it.

Unfortunately, he didn't get it with the Warriors. The team had too many guards and not enough centers. They needed room in their budget to sign a taller player. On December 9, just over a year since Jeremy had made his NBA debut with Golden State, the team cut him.

The owner was hurt but had to make the decision. His teammates wished him well. Stephen Curry sent him a tweet: "Can't say it enough man your work ethic and skills are gonna pick you right back up . . . keep the faith bro and keep ya head up."

Jeremy understood why he had been let go. "That's what I'm understanding through all this—it's a business. It was a calculated business decision they made to benefit the team. I have no hard feelings."

Still, Jeremy must have been sad to have his hometown NBA dream cut off. Once again, he found himself in the tough position of having someone tell him no.

He got a short reprieve when he was signed by the Houston Rockets on December 12. However, they had four guards ahead of him and he was let go again. This time, the Rockets cut him on Christmas Eve.

Little did Jeremy, the Warriors, the Rockets, and the NBA know what was ahead.

Finding a New Home

Jeremy didn't have to wait long to pack his sneakers and get back onto an NBA team. Just two days after Christmas, the New York Knicks signed him to a contract.

Heading into the new 2011–12 NBA season, the Knicks needed some help. Their main starting point guards were an inexperienced

Toney Douglas and an older Mike Bibby. Behind them, veteran Baron Davis was hurt. And rookie Iman Shumpert was injured, too. Jeremy provided insurance for the position.

"I'm just going to play basketball," Lin said Wednesday before his first Knicks shootaround. "I'm not going to overthink anything. I'm just going to go out there, have some fun, and play. I'm thankful that people want me. I understand my position: I'm competing for a backup spot, and people see me as the twelfth guy on the roster. It's a numbers game."

As for the Knicks, they thought they might be able to use a player with Jeremy's skills.

"We liked his speed, we liked his aggressiveness, we liked his size, we liked him being able to penetrate," Coach Mike D'Antoni said.

It was a big change for Jeremy. He went from playing on his hometown team to being unemployed to playing in the biggest city in America . . . all in about two weeks in late 2011. It was a shock, he admitted, to be cut by Golden State. But this spot with the Knicks was a welcome relief.

"It seems like forever ago," Lin said about leaving Golden State, "but obviously [the Knicks are] a dream come true. And I'm still excited, just as excited, to be with the Knicks right now."

Jeremy made his debut in a Knicks uniform on the road against his old team, the Warriors. However, the Jeremy Lin who had played his last Warriors game back in April 2010 was not the Jeremy Lin who took the floor in his soon-to-be-famous No. 17 Knicks jersey. The six months between games had given him a chance to remake himself and his game. He was stronger, faster, a better jumper, a purer shooter. He had worked on every part of his game, with coaches and by himself. By the time he got his chance with the Knicks, he was more ready than he'd ever been.

New York put Jeremy into that first regular-season game late and he missed his only shot. He got a nice hand from his old hometown fans but the Warriors beat the Knicks, 92–78. After that game, Coach D'Antoni was not happy. The Knicks' struggles would soon open the door for Jeremy.

"The whole game, our offense was awful," D'Antoni told reporters afterward. "We let opportunities slip by, just because we weren't in sync, we didn't make shots, we turned the ball over, we gave up layups. And we let them hang around until they caught a little bit of fire."

Jeremy showed his team that he was still trying hard to improve. During practice sessions before and after the team workouts, Jeremy spent time with Knicks assistant coach Kenny Atkinson. The pair continued to improve Jeremy's shooting. They spent a lot of time on his passing as well. Jeremy asked for tapes of himself playing to watch for mistakes and to see what he'd done wrong.

Jeremy appeared in four more games for the Knicks in the first month of the season. On January 17, he was sent back to his old stomping grounds: the D-League. Along with center Jerome Jordan, Jeremy went to play for the Erie

BayHawks. He would not be there long. In one game, he had a triple-double: double digits in points (28), rebounds (11), and assists (12). The Knicks were still struggling on offense. It was time to bring back the kid from Harvard.

"Jeremy went to Harvard, so he might be the smartest guy we have," said Coach D'Antoni. "But he's very quick, he defends pretty well, and he can really get in the lane and distribute the basketball."

Soon, the coach would be able to see all those skills in action. Jeremy played just a few minutes in his first game back. Then on January 28, against the Houston Rockets, he was in for almost all of the second half. He played 20 minutes and scored nine points, the most he'd scored in a game since the previous

April. His crisp play opened the coaches' eyes a bit.

He saw action in the team's next two games, a blowout win over the Detroit Pistons and a loss to the Boston Celtics.

It seemed as if he was falling back into the same place he'd been with Golden State—a backup to a backup who spent more time watching than playing.

Meanwhile, Jeremy might have had a team again, but he didn't have a home. Since returning from Erie's D-League team in late January, his living situation had been a little strange. Jeremy didn't have a place in New York City. His brother Josh, who was going to school in the city, came through. He offered his little brother a spot on his living-room couch! While living the high life of an NBA player during the day and evening, when he went "home," Jeremy crashed on the sofa.

And then it all came together.

February 4, 2012, will always be remembered as the day the world went Linsane.

The Knicks were on a tough streak. They had lost 11 of their last 13 games. Their offense was struggling. Their guards were being outplayed. D'Antoni was looking for a spark. Early in the first half of a game against the New Jersey Nets, he called Jeremy's number. It was the right decision.

Jeremy had his best NBA game so far. He ended up playing 36 minutes, more than he had in any game. (He had only played 55 minutes total in the Knicks' first 23 games!) He was doing so well that star Carmelo Anthony suggested to the coach that Jeremy keep playing in the second half. Jeremy ended up scoring 25 points, also his most ever. He was at his best late in the game, scoring 12 of his points in the all-important fourth quarter.

He did all this while also playing tough defense and going up against the Nets' Deron Williams, one of the best players in the NBA. He scored key points late, including a reverse layup that gave the Knicks a four-point lead, and a driving layup through a double-team that helped clinch the win.

The Knicks won 99–92, but all anyone could talk about after the game was this amazing kid from . . . well, out of nowhere!

After being mobbed by his teammates on

the court, Jeremy was just as popular with the media after the game. He sat on his stool in the locker room with microphones all around him and smiled. "This hasn't sunk in yet, I'm still trying to figure this out."

He wasn't the only one. . . .

Jeremy was showing ability that nobody knew he had, including Coach D'Antoni. "We didn't know if he could defend well enough. We didn't know whether he could finish well enough. And we didn't know if he could shoot outside well enough. We did like his playmaking ability. We liked his ability to get in the paint. We liked that he was unselfish. We liked that he was smart. We liked that he had all the intangibles of being a point guard."

The Nets game opened a lot of people's

eyes. By the next day, he was being swarmed by reporters. Other media people were tracking down his old coaches and trying to interview family members in California and Taiwan. Would he be a one-game wonder? Or would this be the start of something big?

Linsanity!

Hold on tight to your book—things are about to get a little crazy.

After Jeremy's great performance against the Nets, he had earned more playing time. Baron Davis was still hurt, and with the Knicks struggling overall, it was time for a change. The fans at the famous Madison Square Garden were calling for more Jeremy.

Next up for the Knicks was the Utah Jazz. Jeremy got his first-ever NBA start, to the delight of the sold-out Garden audience. Jeremy was able to meet some special fans at the game, too. Among the crowd cheering on New York's newest hero was a pack of other recent New York heroes. Several members of the New York Giants were at the game just a few days after winning Super Bowl XLVI.

With star forward Amar'e Stoudemire missing the game due to a death in his family, Jeremy would have his work cut out for him. It didn't get any easier when Carmelo Anthony left the court in the first quarter with an injury. But the lack of offensive firepower was no obstacle for the NBA's newest star. Jeremy pumped in 28 points and had eight assists. He matched up against

Utah's Devin Harris, one of the quickest players in the NBA, and had no problems.

Jeremy did get help from a teammate playing with the big stars out. Rarely used forward Steve Novak had five three-point shots among his career-high 19 points, several of them on assists from Jeremy.

Along with setting up Novak for bombs, Jeremy was beginning to work well with forward Tyson Chandler. On several plays against Utah, he lofted alley-oop passes for Chandler to slam home. Later in the game, Chandler tipped a long rebound to Jeremy that he flung up for a three-point shot just before the 24-second clock ran out. *Swish!*

After the game, reporters poured into the Knicks' locker room to find out more about this surprising hero. As usual, Jeremy wanted to talk about his teammates, not himself. "Basketball's so much fun when you're playing on a team where people want to work together and work through tough times and overcome them and have victories like this," he said.

For his part, Knicks Coach Mike D'Antoni knew a good thing when he saw it. He left Jeremy in the game much longer than the young guard had ever played. "I'm going to ride him like Secretariat," he said, comparing his young star to one of the greatest winners in horse-racing history. "I was going to take him out, and he looked at me and said, 'I don't want to come out.'"

This game really kicked off Linsanity. Jeremy's big performance against the Nets got some headlines, but starting and doing even better in his second game really moved him up the charts. The puns on his name started to fly: Linsanity, Lincredible, He's a Linner, A Linderella Story, The Sky's the Lin-it.

With Linsanity booming around the country and his every move on the front page of dozens of newspapers and sports websites, Jeremy led the Knicks on the road for their next game. They headed south to face the Washington Wizards. That club was led by John Wall, Jeremy's old summer-league foe.

Just as he had in the summer, Jeremy outplayed Wall, scoring 23 points. The Knicks had their third straight win with Jeremy at the controls of the offense. At one point, Jeremy blew past Wall for a one-handed slam dunk!

"Just one of those in-the-moment things," Lin said about that play. "I think they messed up on their coverage, so I was able to get free."

Jeremy was just showing off the many different skills he had acquired in high school and college. Now he was getting the national spotlight in the NBA. At one point, he faced up a Wizards defender at the top of the key. With a slight hesitation dribble that froze the opponent, Jeremy sliced past for an easy layup. A few minutes later, he floated in an outside shot while falling backward toward the crowd. And he continued to team up with Chandler, tossing him a nice alley-oop pass in the lane. On that night, Jeremy set a new career high with 10 assists. It was a mark that would not last long.

As Jeremy's winning streak reached three,

the teams that he once played for were regretting their choice. "We always felt there would be some chance he'd be a backup point guard," said Larry Riley, the Warriors' general manager. "I have egg on my face in telling you that I did not think he was going to become a starting point guard with a good team. He's doing that right now."

The crowds got louder, the Knicks kept winning, and the attention Jeremy was getting just grew and grew. It had been only a week from his first big game against the Nets until the game on February 10 against the Lakers. But in that time, Jeremy had become the biggest story in sports.

For his part, Jeremy was just trying to stay calm and play his game. He couldn't avoid the attention—he got standing ovations just for going into a restaurant—but he worked hard to keep it from distracting him. Even though he was suddenly a big star, he was still sleeping on his brother's couch.

On February 10, in a battle with scoring star Kobe Bryant and the Lakers, Linsanity got even more amaz-Lin'!

The Lakers had beaten the Knicks the last four times they had visited Madison Square Garden. They came into this game as one of the best teams in the West. Meanwhile, even though the Knicks had won three straight, they still had a losing record. It would not have been a surprise if the Lakers swamped the Knicks, especially with Stoudemire and Anthony still out.

But Jeremy was determined to keep winning. Led by his stunning 38 points (Kobe had just 34!), the Knicks thrilled the Garden crowd by upsetting the Lakers. It was a triumph for Jeremy, just another example of his continued success in the face of adversity.

He wasted no time making his mark in the game. He scored the Knicks' first points with a three-point rainbow from the corner. A few minutes later, his no-look pass to Chandler led to a bucket. Then he stole the ball at midcourt and started a one-man fast break for two points.

His best play of the night came late in the second quarter. Facing the Lakers' ace defender, veteran guard Derek Fisher, Jeremy did a complete 360-degree spin, went past Fisher, and floated in a layup. The Garden crowd went nuts.

Jeremy matched Miami star LeBron James as the only players in the NBA with four games of 20 points and seven assists in the 2011–12 season. Jeremy's 89 points in his first three starts also was the most by any player since 1976.

After the Lakers game, two-time NBA MVP Steve Nash of Phoenix, one of Jeremy's role models as a point guard, tweeted, "If you love sports, you have to love what Jeremy Lin is doing."

Jeremy's teammates agreed. "The confidence he plays with, the understanding of the game, he's taken us all by surprise. Not only us, but the whole league right now," said Tyson Chandler.

His teammates were in awe of his hot streak. "After the first game, it was, 'Wow, he played great,'" Novak said. "After the second game, it was 'Wow, he's really stepping up.' After the third game, he started making believers out of everyone. After this game, I know it's early. But he keeps getting better every game. It's real. I'm saying in the next game, he might score fifty. I feel like I'm a part of history."

Jeremy, of course, just kept smiling and playing hard. But he wasn't going to let all the attention change who he was. "It's a once-in-a-lifetime opportunity," he told a pack of cameras and microphones. "I'm going to play as long as I can. I'm going to enjoy this. When I look back, I'm going to say I gave it all I could."

The great Kobe Bryant knew that Jeremy was not a fluke. It was just his time to shine. "When a player is playing that well, he doesn't come out of nowhere. It seems like he comes out of nowhere. Go back and take a look, and the skill level was probably there from the beginning, it's just that we didn't notice it."

Meanwhile, fans in other places were enjoying this Lincredible story, too. His grandmother who took care of him as a child was still watching. Although she lived back in Taiwan, she never missed one of Jeremy's games, much like millions of people in that proud country. Most of them, however, understand more than she does about what her grandson is accomplishing.

"I know nothing about basketball. I only know when Jeremy puts the ball in the basket he has done a good thing," she told the *New York Times*. Jeremy's uncle Lin Chi Chung told a *Times* reporter that he had to keep working during the Knicks–Raptors game, but everyone around him had iPads . . . so he could keep track of the score easily.

Jeremy's high school was in the Lin-light, too. Everyone wanted to hear what it had been like to coach this sudden star. "It's been crazy for me," Diepenbrock says. "I can't imagine what it's like to be him."

It was getting pretty crazy pretty quickly. The wordplay on his name was everywhere: Linsational; Just Lin, Baby; Va-Lin-tine's Day. Jeremy said that his personal favorite was Super Lintendo, since he was such a video-game fan.

"The whole thing has been overwhelming for me and my family," Lin told *Sports Illustrated*. "There are lots of times when we have to pinch ourselves and ask, Is this really happening?"

It was really happening, Jeremy . . . and it wasn't over. Madison Square Garden ran out of Lin merchandise after two nights. They had to iron his number —17— to T-shirts just to have a few more to sell to rabid fans.

The night after the Lakers win—and after a long flight to Minnesota—the Linsane Train just kept rolling. Jeremy scored 15 points in the first half, but then struggled in the second half, making just one of 13 shots.

But he kept working hard. Late in the game as the Knicks tried to get back into it, he dribbled around and under three Timberwolves to bank in a short shot. Then with New York trailing with 39 seconds left, Jeremy found Novak, who hit a long three-pointer. But it wasn't over yet. That just tied the game at 98–98. After a Minnesota turnover, it was time for Jeremy to shine again. He drove the lane and was fouled as he tried to shoot. That meant he got two free throws. Amazingly, the first one clanged off the rim!

No problem. He calmly made the second with just 4.9 seconds left. New York stopped a desperate final play and put another *W* in the books.

Jeremy was exhausted after the game. He had not played this much basketball in one stretch since college. He had to ice down his legs for a while before he could talk with reporters. Of course, it was not a big surprise what he said. "I feel like I'm in a dream right now. What a win. What a gutsy team win. I can't say enough. I love playing for this team. These guys are just so unselfish."

How big was Jeremy and his Linderella story? After his first week of full-time NBA action, he was the cover story in *Sports Illustrated*. He was named NBA Player of the Week for February 6–12. And the Knicks, who had lost 11 of 13 games before Jeremy, were suddenly the hottest team in the NBA.

As for Jeremy Lin, he was the hottest athlete in any sport . . . in the world.

He's Lincredible!

ith a five-game winning streak, the Knicks were on a roll. But that was nothing compared to the international Linsanity caused by Jeremy's success.

Why was he so popular? Well, his success on the court was a huge part of it. But perhaps a bigger part was his story. As we've seen, he really didn't come from nowhere. He's been a star almost everywhere he's played. But he didn't travel the usual path of an NBA star. He didn't play at a big basketball college, and he wasn't a high draft pick. Whenever a player doesn't follow the "usual" path, and still succeeds, people are amazed.

Jeremy's heritage made him unique, too. The attention he got from the Asian-American community that started in high school expanded enormously. TV stations interviewed Asian-American fans all over who were extremely excited about Jeremy's success. They saw him as a role model for making it where very few Asian-Americans had succeeded. In the major sports of football, baseball, and basketball, the number of top Asian-American players is tiny.

Jeremy felt very happy and blessed to be supported by so many people. For him, the best part was the energy that the full-house crowds gave him, whether the fans were Asian-American or not.

For people in Asia itself, especially in the Lin family's home nation of Taiwan, it was Linsane. Millions gathered around their TVs early in the morning to watch the Knicks' games (when it is evening in New York City, it is morning in Taiwan). His every move was front-page news and the lead story on TV newscasts. On weibo, a top social media site in China, the number of people following Jeremy, whose name in Chinese is actually Lin Shu-Hao, went from 150,000 to 1.4 million in a week . . . and is still climbing!

"Lin is an inspiration," a student named Zou Jiachen told the *Los Angeles Times*. "I saw on a TV documentary that he works from morning to night."

The NBA was paying close attention to it all, too. For more than a decade, the league had been trying to grow the game in Asia. NBA teams have played there, players have visited to show off their skills, and basketball shoe companies have sold gear all over. Several Chinese players have made it to the NBA, the most famous being Yao Ming. The recently retired superstar, who had met Jeremy when he invited the young star to Taiwan for a charity hoops game, was watching closely, too.

"Fans here in China are very excited about Jeremy Lin," Yao said. "He is news all over the place. His story is always on the cover page of the newspaper now. He is not drafted. He signs a minimum contract. In his first year he barely gets minutes to play. Then he gets a chance and in one night he owns New York.

"Since the NBA games are on in the morning because of the time difference in China, you wake up every day and you want to see what he did. What was the score? What were his points and assists? Every day the excitement grows. They win again! Where does the story go next?"

"Everybody thinks it's crazy in the U.S.," Cheng Ho, a friend of Jeremy's who works for the NFL in China, told *Sports Illustrated*. "But it's a much bigger storm here in China. And it's just beginning."

Back in the United States, the Linsanity took over every type of media. There were thousands of blog posts, millions of tweets, articles in every paper in the country. TV crews jostled for his attention. Reporters tracked down everyone who had ever known Jeremy or played with or against him. His whole life was covered from his first dribbles to his latest meals. TV crews showed up to watch his brother Joseph play hoops for Hamilton College.

According to a company that measures social media, Jeremy was mentioned more often during his first amazing week than any other NBA player . . . and more than President Barack Obama! And even the president himself, a big hoops fan, was watching. He talked with his staff about Jeremy's wonderful run. He also said that he had heard of Jeremy long before most people. Like Jeremy, President Obama went to Harvard. So he had been following his fellow Crimson's success for years.

It went beyond just Jeremy, too. The stock of the company that owns Madison Square Garden went up more than 11 percent in his first week of action. His rookie basketball card sold for more than $21,000. Stores all over New York were selling Lin gear as fast as it could be made. One store signed up several new factories to churn out shirts, hats, and more.

After only a week, Jeremy had the top-selling jersey in the NBA. And after two weeks in the NBA, he was on back-to-back covers of *Sports Illustrated*. In the 58-year history of that famous magazine, no other New York City athlete had ever done that.

But through it all, Jeremy just played his game. He knew what was going on around him. He saw the headlines and the signs people made at games. He was busy tweeting, too, telling fans what he was doing and thanking them for their support and "energy." But as his friends and family said, he just remained Jeremy, the levelheaded young man they had known for years. Jeremy called on that family support as he became a major overnight celebrity.

How He Got Here

o while new hoops fans jumped on the bandwagon, experts were wondering how they had missed noticing Jeremy for more than a year. As Kobe Bryant had said after his team was beaten by Jeremy and the Knicks, Jeremy didn't really come out of nowhere. But he was just now getting his first real chance to show his skills.

It starts with his energy.

"I just try to play as hard as I can every possession," Lin said. "If you're aware and you're high-energy, the ball will eventually bounce your way and you'll be able to make plays."

Jeremy's reactions on the court spread a lot of excitement. He looks like he is having fun while playing the game, which gets the fans excited. He is just as jazzed when a teammate makes a key shot.

Jeremy also has a high basketball IQ. That means he plays with intelligence. He studies the game before, during, after. He uses his mind and his imagination as much as his jump shot and dribble.

His high school coach, Pete Diepenbrock, sees that in the grown-up Jeremy. "He knows exactly what needs to be done at every point in the . . . game. He's able to exert his will on basketball games in ways you would not expect."

Others see his growth physically. Jeremy's trainer from the lockout days, Phil Wagner, has said about Jeremy's transformation from then to now: "The biggest thing I see is when he gets into traffic [on the court], he's able to maintain his direction and his balance, because he's stronger. He's a physical guard. That's where I see his hard work and the program he did with us paying off. Before, he was a motorcycle: He was maneuverable, but very off-balance. Now he's like a Porsche: He's fast, but he's stable."

There's that hard work again. At every stop along his basketball journey, Jeremy has made hard work a big part of his life. Before practice, at practice, during the season, between seasons—it's all about working to improve.

Jeremy describes himself as being "a playmaker. I'm always attacking the rim and have somewhat of a reckless style. I try to be everywhere at once."

Harvard assistant coach Kenny Blakeney spelled out some of the key basketball skills that have helped turn Jeremy from a good player into a star player. As the coach explained to *Sports Illustrated*, Jeremy has great control of his body. He can start and stop in a very small space. He is excellent at finding space between players. This helps him drive to the basket or find lanes to pass in. The coach also praised Jeremy's dribbling skills. He said that the young man he knew at Harvard could go any direction almost instantly.

Finally, Jeremy's mental strength is a big part of his game. As NBA veteran Yao Ming put it, "What I see from Jeremy and what I hear in his interviews is he appreciates everything. He pursues his dream. His attitude is so peaceful, but there is strength to him. It is not a violent strength like fire or something aggressive. It is like the ocean, very peaceful, very quiet when you look at it. But you can never underestimate the power that is in there."

Put it all together—the hard work, the basketball smarts, the mental and physical growth, and the on-court skills—and you find that Jeremy Lin didn't just pop up overnight. He's been a star in the making since his dad handed him a basketball.

Another Linstallment

In a game on Valentine's Day, Jeremy put a mighty cap on his week-plus of excitement with his biggest play yet.

The Knicks traveled to Canada to play the Toronto Raptors. The Raptors were hot in the first half, leading by as many as 17 points. But Jeremy led the Knicks right back. New York still trailed by five with 90 seconds left. Then

Iman Shumpert made a steal and a layup. Down by three, Jeremy drove the lane a moment later. He made a tough basket and was knocked to the floor. He made the foul shot to tie the score!

He was not done. A few moments later, with 20,000 people on their feet in Toronto and time running out, Jeremy calmly dribbled near the top of the key. The clock ticked down . . . 5, 4, 3, 2 . . . he rose up and let fly—*swish!* A buzzer-beating three-pointer to win the game! Even the opposing Toronto crowd cheered his performance.

All that "Beat the Ghost" with Doc Scheppler had paid off. After Jeremy buried that game-winning three, one of the first things he did was send a text to his mentor. "Doc, that was all you," Lin wrote. "Thanks for everything you did for me."

"I'm thankful that the coach and my team-mates trust me with the ball at the end of the game," Jeremy then told reporters. "I like having it at the end of the game. I'm just very thankful."

"You just watch and you're in awe," D'Antoni said. "He held it until five tenths of a second left. He was pretty confident that was going in, no rebounds, no nothing. That ball was buried."

After six wins in a row for Jeremy and the Knicks, the records just kept piling up. Jeremy's 136 points in his first five starts were the most since the NBA and ABA (American Basketball Association) merged in 1976. He became only the third Knick ever to have six straight games with 20 points and seven assists. And the Knicks have been playing since 1947!

In the Knicks' next game, against the Sacramento Kings, Jeremy didn't score as much—only 10 points—but his work helped seven Knicks reach double figures in points. Showing how much he was learning even as he kept winning, Jeremy said, "As a point guard, my field-goal attempts have been really high and I don't think that's necessarily good," Lin said. "I think it's more of my job to distribute and get people in rhythm."

On the other team's bench was a familiar face. Former Golden State Coach Keith Smart now ran the Kings. He remembered the young man he had coached only a year earlier. "I knew him before Linmania. He's still the same humble guy. The guy has not changed a bit, which is real special for a young man."

The Knicks won 100–85 and the "Linning" streak was at seven games. The wins not only made Jeremy a household name, they evened the Knicks' record at 15–15. Against the New Orleans Hornets on February 17, however, the streak finally ended. Jeremy scored 26 points, but he also had nine turnovers and the Knicks lost 89–85. Turnovers were starting to be a problem. The 45 he had in his first five games, like the points, were the most by a player since 1976. With less than a minute left, he tried to force a shot on a drive but missed badly. Was Jeremy starting to try a little bit too hard and take too much on himself?

"It was just a lackluster effort on my part

coming out and [being] careless with the ball," Jeremy said after the game. "Nine turnovers is obviously never gonna get it done from your primary ball-handler. It's on me in terms of taking care of the ball and the game in general. If everyone's going to credit me for these last seven games, then I definitely deserve this one. So that's fine by me."

Linsanity took a bit of a breather with the loss, but it was a short one. Two days later, the Knicks took on the defending NBA champion Dallas Mavericks. A new Knicks player, J.R. Smith, joined the team after finishing play in the China Basketball Association. Smith had done what Jeremy was also offered—played in China during the lockout. Smith hit three three-point shots in the first quarter, and Jeremy capped off that first period with a jumper at the buzzer. Dallas came back, however, and held the lead in the third quarter.

Jeremy started a comeback with a powerful drive through traffic to cut the lead to nine. A few minutes later, he made a steal and a slam dunk to cut the Mavs' lead to just one. A trio of Novak three-pointers put the Knicks ahead. Jeremy sunk his own long-range shot to build a nine-point lead. Dallas got as close as three points, but the last of Jeremy's career-high 14 assists, a long pass to Anthony, clinched it. The Knicks had another win!

In a loss to the Nets the following evening, Jeremy scored 20 points for the ninth time. He also had a season-high seven rebounds plus four steals. But Deron Williams was determined not to let Lin take over the game again as he did in his first breakout performance against the Nets 16 days earlier. Willams scored 38 points and the Nets ended up ahead 100–92.

Jeremy and the Knicks bounced back with a win over the Atlanta Hawks on February 22. He only had 17 points, but that was tied for the team high. He also had nine big assists. One of the most spectacular was a long rainbow pass down the court. Carmelo Anthony caught it in stride and slammed it home. The Knicks led by as many as 28 before winning 99–82. That made it nine wins in 11 games since Jeremy came off the bench against the Nets only 18 days earlier.

With the All-Star break approaching, the Knicks had one more game before the league took a long weekend off. Unfortunately for the Knicks, that one more game was against the best team in the NBA, the Miami Heat. And Jeremy, perhaps tired after so many games in a row, had his worst game as a Knick. He only made one basket, though he was six-for-six in free throws. He also had eight turnovers and only three assists. The mighty Heat, led by LeBron James, Dwyane Wade, and Chris Bosh, swarmed over the Knicks 102–82.

Though that was a tough loss to end the first half of the season, Jeremy could point with great pride at what he'd done. Less than a month earlier, the Knicks had been seven games under .500. Since February 4, they had gone 9–3 and created a tone of positive buzz among their fans.

As for the All-Star Weekend itself, thanks

to all the excitement about his miracle season, Jeremy was invited to take part in the Rising Stars Challenge. That game was between a group of rookie and sophomore players and Jeremy was picked third out of all the players included. Trying to get some rest, Jeremy didn't play much in the game, but he did enjoy working with the team's "General Manager," Shaquille O'Neal.

"I had posters of Shaq on my walls when I was a kid," Jeremy said with a smile. As big a star as he had become, Jeremy was still a fan.

The 2012 All-Star Weekend in Orlando was a big change from the 2011 All-Star Weekend in Los Angeles. Back then, even though he was a player for the Warriors at the time, Jeremy had volunteered to work. He helped players and staff during the Skills Challenge. He also went to the dunk contest and the game . . . but with a ticket.

In 2012, he was an honored guest, the biggest story on a weekend packed with big names.

What's Next?

y now, we've seen how Jeremy and the Knicks did after the All-Star break (Mike D'Antoni stepped down as coach of the Knicks after a tough six-game losing streak). But what might be most important is what he will do in the many seasons to come. Can he continue to show the world the amazing young man he is? Jeremy thinks he can do it.

"Everyone is blessed with some sort of talent, but what you also need is drive, focus, hunger, discipline," he told "First Person." "You need those things to be able to use the talent. How close you get to your potential is based on how hard you work."

People know him on the court from his success and skills. But Jeremy wants people to know that he's another guy off the court. His YouTube videos are designed to show off his fun side, his more casual side. On the court, he's a focused, hardworking guy who doesn't let his emotions show too much (unless he's really psyched!). Off the court, he enjoys having fun, but he's also a serious person. Jeremy's faith is very important to him, too.

"I've never really preached before," Lin

says. "But I'm really passionate about Christianity and helping others. There's a beauty in seeing people change their lifestyles for the better."

He uses that faith as a balance while the world knocks constantly on his door.

"I'm not playing to prove anything to anybody," Lin said in an exclusive interview with his hometown *San Jose Mercury News*. "That affected my game last year [in 2011] and my joy last year. With all the media attention, all the love from the fans (in the Bay Area), I felt I needed to prove myself. Prove that I'm not a marketing tool, I'm not a ploy to improve attendance. Prove I can play in this league. But I've surrendered that to God. I'm not in a battle with what everybody else thinks anymore."

Will he stay as popular as he was in his first

handful of games? Only time will tell—time and his success on the court. If Jeremy stops scoring so many points or doesn't play as well, a lot of the attention he has earned might go elsewhere. But as anyone who knows him would say, don't count him out. He's a guy who just doesn't listen when someone tells him "no."

"If he proves himself to be a player for a long time, the sky's the limit for him," David Carter of the USC Sports Business Institute told the *Los Angeles Times*. "He could go from being an underdog to the mighty dog."

His former coach thinks Jeremy's run of success can last. "I think it's for real," D'Antoni said. "The things that are real are his vision, which won't change; his speed, which won't change; his knowledge of the game, which won't change. I think it can only get better."

Eventually teams will figure out how to stop him, such as the Heat did in late February. "I'm sure someone's going to figure out how to slow him down and stop him," said his former assistant coach at Harvard, Lamar Reddicks. "It's a chess match. He's going to figure out how to beat that. That, to me, is a kind of a testament of who he is."

But being stopped will be nothing new to Jeremy Lin. He's been stopped, overlooked, ignored, and shut down over and over. But he just keeps working, keeps believing, and keeps moving forward.

Sure, it helps that he's a really talented player. But without that hard work and that confidence, he wouldn't be Linsane!

Author's Note

The author would like to thank the reporters and writers from the following publications and websites: The *New York Times*, *San Jose Mercury News*, *New York Daily News*, *San Francisco Chronicle*, *Los Angeles Times*, *The Age*, *Washington Post*, *Orange County Register*, *USA Today*, *Harvard Crimson*, *Sports Illustrated*, *Time*, NBA.com, ESPN.com, SI.com, basketball-reference.com.